73

DEADNAME

ABHAINN CONNOLLY

WWW.WRITEBLOODYUK.CO.UK

First edition.
ISBN 978-1-8380332-7-9

Typeset by Angelo Maneage
Cover by Choirstaidh NicArtair
Edited and Proofread by Fern Beattie
Author Photo by Beth Tucker

Typeset in Bergamo & Arial

Write Bloody UK • London, UK

Support Independent Presses
WWW.WRITEBLOODYUK.CO.UK

DEADNAME

CONTENTS

DEAD

[REDACTED]

NAME

ACKNOWLEDGMENTS

For Poppy

DEAD

Ó táimse in aimsir ag an mbás,
is baolach ná beidh mé saor riamh uaidh.

Nuala Ní Dhomnaill, "Mo Mháistir Dorcha"

I've hired myself out to death. And I'm afraid that I'll not ever be let go.

translated by Paul Muldoon

ODE TO MY DYING NAME

A gender always enters the room before me. You,
her chariot. You, the divine saddle, worn leather,
cool buckle that taught her a thigh's grip.
The gift of my mother's middle; the sound that
pulled me awake in the aftermath of the car crash
on Interstate 25, golden & wide, a rising butter sun
of *she's alive*. You are the word my lovers used
in specific sacred praise to my hands, a thirty-four-year acre
to call home. Will I know who I am
without you?

Many days you were the only thing that stood
between me & the vast, incredible nothing –
the times they accused me of not understanding
my place. I was you when I was loving her
like a northern summer sunset, staying awake
until I squeezed all the light the highest season
allowed. You subtitled this soft body that welcomed
the spread of its skin to the wrong women, yet offered
the staircase inside me to hide from the blows.
I always responded as you when somebody else

wanted something. And though you have always been
beautiful, you have never been
mine. Let it be known that there's only one name
to which I will answer now – not the letter name –
but the self that has spoken and said:
I have finally arrived.
I have come to be seen and heard.
I am choosing what only I can.

MISOPHONIA, OR HOW TO BE TRANS & BE QUIET

I hate unclean sounds: sloppy ones from
those who have the privilege of breathing
or eating like being alive is not a big secret to keep.
The nuns used to soak a washrag & force it
over the corners of my mouth after lunch,
hold the back of my head like a hook in the gills
while I went stiff & bucked,

> *why*
> *can't*
> *you*
> *act*
> *like*
> *a*
> *lady?*

I learned to lick my face & plate spotless.
Do everything through my nose, which cannot
say the wrong thing. Being unsafe, I learned, has a
smell. I swallowed the coin of keeping
my mouth closed like the good neighbour girls
who were never sent out to play with bodies of
social tender. Imagine my gender
did not belong to the highest bidder.
Imagine I was known before I was collateral
for a good Catholic home. Imagine I believed
in being loved & heard by the same people,
that I am not some dykeboi who now dreams
of cutting their stomach fat straight off the bone
for a chance at getting misgendered
in the opposite direction. Then I might like
things to make a sound. I might sit
in the corner, my jaw angled like a ladle,
& slurp the leftovers of my meals
from my nail beds, no longer afraid
of anyone noticing. Maybe then
they would all use
the right pronoun.

THE BLADE IS MEANT TO COMFORT

Someday, I will never see you again. That is the truest thing
I could ever write. I feel wholly unprepared to usher you into
a passing you won't understand. Spoiler alert; the dog dies.
My shadow for weeks and months and years is insufficient.

Sometimes we are the blade. We are asked to decide if someone
should live or die. At the same time we have no say in anything
at all. Either way, we are asked to be precise.

THIS HAS A NAME

I.   I lose my wallet in NYC and call you. You tell me you have it, but that it is empty. Earlier, you walk out on me in a restaurant without a word in the middle of an argument. I text you *this behavior has a name and it isn't cool* and you say that *isn't what is happening* and I don't bother to tell you *that* has a name, too.

II.   You don't storm out of the restaurant. You ask to read one of my poems, like you used to, and I am excited. You finish it and shrug, pass back my phone, tell me you miss your dog.

III.   We go to the airport and I ask a flight attendant if she's seen my wallet. She doesn't respond. She swats her ear. She asks if anyone wants the seat next to you. No one can see me sitting there. I pinch myself. You look at me like I am embarrassing you. I stop checking.

HE ISN'T THERE

Instead, the Prius drives itself. I am a quiet
passenger. The air conditioning hugs me to the soft seat.
We go the perfect speed to swipe right on all the tides
of sugar beets in their rowed swells. The Prius asks me questions.
Tell me what your book is about. What is the first thing you dream of
right after you plug in your phone and roll over. Will your
dog accept strawberries. I am wearing my most comfortable
black joggers, the ones Google told me were for androgyny
with thicker thighs and I feel like a boy from below my last
rib, for once. Then, my dad is driving and I know to shut up.
I have been meaning to ask you, he says, *do you feel like your life is*
going downhill, backwards. A bug gives its guts to the windshield
and I envy its trajectory. I don't know how to answer him. I am literally
in a metal box that can roll me anywhere, even up hills. I am going
to an airport to get on a bigger one that will bypass the hills altogether.
Proportionately, we only ever back these things up a little
and then go more forward. I consult the navigation.
We are both heading in the same direction, but only one of us
likes who I am.

WHAT'S A POPPER

A good idea is touching your tits so you know it can feel good.
The last three lovers grabbed mine too hard, like they owned

them, so it is important to show my tits the truth of belonging;
it does not hurt, it has the right hold. When you take testosterone

and start working out, your biceps stop fitting in your old button downs.
Everyone thinks what happens is you want to lob off your tits,

let them fall to the floor next to the lace panties you are supposed to
also no longer want. I have experienced enough heartbreak to know

that I am apt to want to keep the wrong things. Unlike when I was a dyke,
I cannot fuck anyone into believing I am trans. Not even myself.

I feel like I am doing a bad job at this. Like, isn't it embarrassing that a straight person
taught me what poppers are? All this time, I thought I had to open everything up

on my own or force things down. Turns out, you can give something a sniff
and be ready for anything. Take it in like you were born right.

THE NIGHTS OF LOST CAUSE

In advance, know I wanted love without uncertainty.
Like everyone else, I wanted love like I wanted an object,
a mindless permanence.
I would bring anything into the house & keep it as long as it stayed.

Jo left for groceries & the rain fell harder than it had all year.
I placed the last call I'd make on my own phone
& a car arrived carrying my rescuers - those who saw this reckless mind
& were still there to hold me,
my friends. The space between who they knew me to be
& who I was now stared at us,
making sound after sound,
a tender-throated prey-thing pulled from a jaw.

Glorious windfall. Unknowable chimes in the air.
That day was the first day of my freedom - how it has spoken to me again & again
in its ephemeral bliss. Somewhere on the other side of this ample time & its distance,
I am not a survivor.
I was not carried to a safe house,
did not need a new computer.
Somewhere, I am not worried that I no longer know where she lives,
& if it is here. I said every prayer on those nights
of lost cause & each year I will
pray again. This is wonderful,

or is it sad?
I have a hard time believing a lot of things now,
a harder time being believed. But if this is naive, I beg you;
let me be this. Let me remain this version of me
that feels the right things are possible. For this is what it is like
to write about living, or what it is like to feel it again. And what if
the ruin suits me?

LOVE DOESN'T HURT

A slick sound comes from the television.
Ooo-woop! followed by a pitter patter.
A humanoid dog, oval eyes and a turtleneck,
steps on a cartoon banana peel.

A lively jingle accompanies the fall.
Nobody in the house is watching anymore.
Nobody is there. I didn't mean to leave,
but memory is the devil I know.

My condition is a deficit of now.
I call it *post-traumatic* in polite company and
safety when alone. Somewhere parallel,
I am a natural habitat:

the right temperature and precipitation
to sustain life. Zoom out and I am
in the kitchen watching
the glass electric kettle,

tiny LED bubbles being born,
widening their mouths,
lost children of air, until they surface
and burst to their source hunger.

Ooo-woop! again, and the character
is a flurry of arms and legs,
leaning this way and that,
a desperate comedy of upright.

Somewhere parallel,
she is fistful of a viscous rage, seeping
from between her fingers. Isn't it funny
the thoughts we have

when we think we are going to die?
I see again an old commercial through
a television with wire ears – *love doesn't hurt*,
it says – a man and woman

in a physical fight. We look nothing like them:
two queers, one who had shown me
the knife she kept in her pocket earlier in the day, *our secret*,
one of so many secrets,

ramming her fist into a door I am barely holding shut.
I laugh, then and now – the surrender kind,
a series of agonal breaths, laughter that doesn't belong here
or there, like me, neither or both,

here and there. It looks, from the outside,
like waiting on hot water to make tea.
It feels, from the inside, like
slipping and landing somewhere else entirely.

YOU YOU YOU OUGHTA KNOW

You learned very young that thin, fine hair will not stick up
like the horsetail of your brother's scalp. So this is your haircut,

forever. Yesterday you told me you never imagined yourself
much older, couldn't envision what that would look like, so you still sport

that emo shag like a fifty-something Dealz Justin Bieber.
This is why it is becoming harder to ask you to be free

with me. Some people age but never grow. Tickets to Aruba
were $200 today and your life is a lead hand around my throat.

I was once told that you can know someone's age if they use
a wash rag and have hand soap in their kitchen. I know who you're grooming

from your playlists. I watch you cut songs from the one you made me and
they fall like my curls on the salon floor the day I finally tell you I'm going

everywhere without you. I like to imagine you at the barber's one day,
looking at the silk of your hair, dead-indicator of 2006, and saying

Cut it, all of it. Off with your head. Your tongue turns to feathers.
Your jaw breaks the next time you say the word *love*.

WHAT KIND OF SALESMAN ARE YOU

Have you ever convinced yourself
They are the worst thing to happen to you
And the only thing you need
Right now
I see my bedside table
Emptied of the bag of Swedish fish
My painting replaced in the frame
With a picture of them and
Six of their friends on a ski slope
I have to ask you, Reader
If you've ever told yourself
You like the rain better
And then spent eight months
Without the sun
Are you that kind of salesman
A sodden clod at your own door
Telling yourself you can earn back the time
You gave them
And the time
You'll now never know
A snakeskin you twist
In a screaming skillet
When it is obvious
Your heart is only buying it
Because it doesn't yet realize
You are the one
Who broke it

10/10 WOULD KISS WHEN GETTING STOLEN OUT OF REHAB

This is how you've been taken from places before / Downloading Tinder ill-advised and unwell / already coated in her favorite color / a handful of the desert she has never smelled / in your hands / That week, you picked flowers / yellow, purple, a sprig of green reed / things in September that grow / only by saccharine, fluorescent seed / You dip your index and middle finger into an open jar of acrylic / stir as it laps up past your first knuckle / You paint her something that looks like another 30 days / on the right side of yourself / When she picks you up you pretend not to mind /the trash on the floor of the passenger side of her car / the dirt on the seat / how everything reeks of cat piss / The bouquet you bring her sucks up the dust on the dash / its reflection clipped by a wandering crack in the window / that will grow, unattended, this winter /Later, you describe how she seems so afraid of desire / that she cannot feel it / while you are freshly weaned from its raw source / She hovers her lips above yours and you practice saying no / to something numb / What can I tell you about not kissing someone / when you know you could / About how we are all sick / but only some of us get sent away for it / The road that takes you to rehab / is the same one that shows you out / And love always drives us to madness / prisoners of the first time/ it was taken from us

ON LOSS

We were worried about our weight.
Having found each other, our round bellies yawned
like dogs up from a good nap.
Our skin could be folded, our grips filled with
ourselves, each other.
Our bodies announced themselves
to the grand expansion of space;
we thought this was a bad thing.
We thought we knew something
about loss.

What I would give for a handful of you.
What I would give to have the body
that held our raucous laughter:
you dancing in a Santa hat, my crass observations
of each astrological sign. Since you died,
I've become a gaunt vessel for breath,
a city of caves. What I would do
to have my fill of moments beside you,
never getting enough, my body a growing boy
we both encourage to eat.

THIS IS WHAT LOVE IS

The neglected houseplant, weathering
my fierce depression, takes the water I manage to share
from the glass I'd gotten myself and forgotten
three nights ago, and the next day it sends out a bloom.
This maddening loyalty: a dedication. An abundant feeling,
for sure. But rare.

Why couldn't I have settled for you? How often
did I go through the house shutting the windows
at the simple threat of wind? I didn't know enough
then to be as sorry as I am now, that mercy
would be so difficult to come by. I loved you
so much and mistook that for issuing you a proper apology.
I hope you are happy and think of me
very little.

[REDACTED]

Poetry is where we go to get lost to get found. I wrote, like I have always written, because some part of me wanted to justify my choice to be alive.

ALOK VAID-MENON

L'APPEL DU VIDE

The flies are a generous lesson on space here –

large, and they move like a heavy wit.
I smashed one with the back of a book yesterday.

He did not stand a chance. He appeared, in his final moments,

kind of stupid: a creaking joint asked to wake
in a cold room, a mind before it anchors itself out of a dream.

I felt immediate remorse. There was nowhere for my apology

to go. I paused – *is this what it means for something to be dead?*
I think now of my ex-fiancé, cupped in the hand

of a hammock on the porch, how I wondered in that moment

if I loved her anymore, how I wish that I could stop
asking questions. Stop wondering how *dead* works.

Stop wondering if love *dot dot dot*. She is one year gone

and I face a lifetime of sorry
that she will never hear. Of course this is how *dead* works.

Of course real love is stupid and slow.

Now, I let the flies in our home ram their heads from window
to window. I know that somewhere there's a web. I am leaving something

alive, feeding something hidden. This is how I begin to forgive myself.

POPPY

I.

There will be no funeral for you: the soft circumference
of you in my bed, pressed to my belly, our synchronized breath
a facile rhythm. I will not get to tribute your mouthful

of crooked teeth, your mismatched eyes, the warmth of you
on my calloused palm as I lift you into my arms. When you came home,
a survival's toolkit made flesh, I started counting

your life expectancy: 15-18 years. I thought by the time you died,
I would be old enough to say goodbye well. Instead,
that year has arrived, & I grab a handful

of your fur & shove my face into the warm curl of your body,
knowing I do not know how to use a hatchet
at all.

II.

One summer, I drove to a girl's house,
skin lathered in coconut sunscreen, a dash of white on my nose
that I missed rubbing in. Back then, I wasn't warned of loss,

how it peels itself out from under a burnt love until it is the only part of us left
touching the world, until we can't remember what it felt like to hold something
without hurting.

I don't recall what was said to me that day
about how I was no longer wanted, but I still feel the desolate heat
of unrequited grief. With you, I am glad you will never have to know Gone,

that your life will be filled entirely of me until
it is not. & when it is not, you will not know it. When it is not,
only I will.

VAST AND FORGIVING

It is possible that someday we will love all there is to love:
the pouting porch on which my grandmother sipped
her microwaved coffee after the night rain, for example.
I think this as I wake before my new lover, journal
on the kitchen table in a pane of muted autumn light,
a crow with a peanut in his beak making eye contact,
his toes curled on the fence. He must know this;
we are strangers. And this soft moment of affinity,
in our shared lifetime of tireless, unanswered cawing,
shells at our feet, felt like a romance that began
at the beginning of it all, and was ours
and wasn't all the same. Of course, I could be wrong.
But isn't it a gift to accept what has been freely given?
To suppose in the direction of light? Hold a gaze
for as long as it is offered. Trust until the trust is thick
with blossom or becomes a starving bird. Presume
that we, too, will be met with a memory of ourselves
that is vast and forgiving.

TRANSLUCENT

Assume the non-binary night terror is a wake. Enter the scene:
The Murphy wife brings out the good whiskey & you can feel it burning
on your lips. This informs you that the wake is not yours.

The enby rests with folded palms in the middle of the room. They are 14 years old
& still everyone's *daughter & sister & she her hers*. Them, such a polite thing.
Never correcting. Them: a person & a collective. Feel the weight of that.

Imagine they have always come home on time, so good. This is proof
of worth. Do not forget that they are trans. But not the *right kind*
of trans. The enby can't be understood through a body. There is more:

an essence. Water temple. The enby is either a god or a ghost;
they are something that you can choose whether or not to believe in. They've never be
anything solid. Everyone wants to nail down their flesh, to get it.

The trans youth was found hung from the cross beams
of a spare bedroom. From the pulpit, everyone says it was the work of queerness
& not a comment on language. Our enby could've been called anything.

As each person leaves The Murphy's, they look at you and say, *We just don't know
how this could happen. She was such a beautiful young girl.* And here, at the end,
the enby is free from the coffer of being gotten.

CAR TATTOO

Where does the blame start? The text message, *may I please have,*
the delivery team, the two fingers in the little baggie (who manufactured
the baggie?), pillreport.com (this one is safe, it says), his dog

who lay with its head & paw dangled delicately over
the couch - watching. Was it the water's fault, the thing that propelled
the throat? The cones of the eyes, the spreading prickle of skin from spine to the

cushioned handles around his middle, the body's response? I could blame
every moment that passed, is passing, will pass - not a minute surviving
my suspicious eye, not a man would live or has lived or is living

who did not kill my friend. You killed him, you reading this now,
& would you be able to forgive yourself, knowing this? I can't. I told him,
remember your comedowns are horrible

& look where I am, tossing a handful of dirt over the hole he came down into,
hungry ghost pupils showing up for the wake, having received the news over
a drink procured with a fake ID. After I got the call,

I turned to my new mate & said, *they just told me my friend killed*
himself, & the statement was swallowed into the swirling gut
of the party. I thought, *ah sure look, he wouldn't want to kill the party tonight* too

& made another margarita. I didn't know what killed meant. Today, I write
another *Happy birthday, Chris* on a memorialized Facebook page. His sister's son
smiles at me like he's about to invite me out for a banger.

His '66 Camaro is inked on my forearm & an American man in Tesco wants to discuss
the benefits of the engine with me, but I know nothing about cars.
I eventually have to tell him it is my dead friend's headstone,

that we still take the same pills & my arms & legs are graveyards
for my friends. I look at him like he did it all to me
by asking.

CUIR OIDEACHAS AR DO MHAC
(EDUCATE YOUR SONS)

It is New Year's Eve and the television asks us to notice time. We are paused
in our grief. The snow of crêpe drifts down over the city and conceals

the darkness like a silk yellow moon. Icy limbs of destitution have long held our
   neighborhood
in a cold rigor mortis. Inside our room, I cry. What about,

if not everything? Will wildfire swallow my mother's home? Why was my nextdoor
   neighbor
gunned down in her tattoo shop up the street? Did I give my lover the cough

that has kept them from work for weeks? Where do we go when home
is where it hurts? We have to wake up somewhere. My partner will be the one

who has to buy my casket if I am caught in the wrong body
at the wrong grocery store. I feel like I need to apologize every time I leave

the house, as I risk sending my loved ones' lives to my creditors. Don't they know
there are no New Years anymore? Only the start of another quarter for people with

more money than us. They will ask us to freshen our hope two days after the next fune
Our hope pays their bills. We keep attempting to breaststroke through our tar sorrow,

stay afloat, become meals of melancholia, chewed with thick tongues of right & wrong
We think we are what is beautiful about being devoured: worthy of consumption.

In the morgue, there's a red halo around another man's lips. On our screens,
another sad story about his hunger. Somewhere, there's a father watering his sapling so

with blood, growing a boy that will soon need bodies to feed on.

DOLLY PARTON WOULDN'T CALL
HERSELF A FEMINIST

They tell us how bad it is that we use synthetics. *Look at these fibers*
in your lungs, look at your bellies now that it's easier to get food, look
what's in the food that's easy to get, remember that straw
extending the tortoise nostril into the boardrooms of Food & Beverage?

When I was a teenager, I had a friend who loved vegetables, would eat
baby carrots while I heated up Top Ramen on the stove. I was so envious -
how do you get to love things like that? Things that are good
for you? I never met her father, neither did she. My dad would wake us up

after sleepovers on Sunday and bake us a can of cinnamon rolls, orange
flavored. We couldn't eat them without stories of my grandfather welling
up as soft liquid moons under my dad's eyes, the way my own father is welling
up in mine as I write this. Incredible. I get to love

something like that. Our trash can was filled with recyclables
because they hadn't blamed us for the world dying
yet. Dolly Parton won't call herself a feminist but
my mother put her on the record player while we bleached the sinks

in our socks and underwear, and when she was angry with my father
after work. My body was filling rooms with its questions,
I was running from the fights at night,
they kept telling me I was in trouble at school when I learned

to make eye contact. But some mornings
I woke up and smelled cinnamon and oranges - some mornings
I still do.

A MODERN MIRACLE

I invent a tiny tube, a long and thin thing,

so thin you almost can't see it but

a surgeon can see it, with their pupils needled under the bright lights of the
operating room

and they can feel it ever-so-slightly between their trained and latexed fingers.

Here is how it works: one side of the tube is placed between my lips,

not being a surgeon, I can't really feel it, but I inhale and inhale and inhale
when they tell me to

and I hear the doctor whisper, "What an invention, what a feat," as the hissing
in the room grows

louder, a light whistling accompaniment as they thread the other end into a hole in

my sister's skull. I have practiced for this, holding my breath

since the CT scans, of course, all of us have, and the invention nudges itself through

the pink pillowed rows, "Excuse me, pardon me,"

very polite so as not to be noticed, a trait I was good at imparting onto

the tiny tube, why I was such a great inventor, another genetic thing,

and I am turning red, but I know if I keep trying

it will work, I have done all of the tests, I have gotten it all approved, I never miss
a thing, we will collect

all the extra little bundles of cells

and we will put them in a petri dish to laugh at later,

and I will say to my sister, *I told you if I could take this from you, I would,*

and I did, and aren't we exhaling now.

MOURNINGS

We always wake to each other;
my fingernails barely peek from their own beds
and dig through her wire fur to the sweet spot
under her collar. I call her *Poppy*
because when she was born, she bloomed
from a solitary stalk, shared her love
with the ease of a milky sap. She fell
down the stairs again last week and holds
her leg like a broken strand of straw as she walks.
The vet has checklists she fills, prepares
his needles. I pick her up in my arms to calm
her and she breaks out in flower,
sepals dropping as her petal body
unfolds. Before I know it, she will no longer be
burdened by her own weight, and I will be
left scratching out each sweet morning thereafter
for the both of us.

NAME

You must learn one thing.
The world was made to be free in.

Give up all the other worlds
except the one to which you belong.

Sometimes it takes darkness and the sweet
confinement of your aloneness to learn

anything or anyone
that does not bring you alive

is too small for you.

DAVID WHYTE

TO MY FAVORITE EX

I have forgotten how to care
about good people's youthful failures.
We were trying to figure it out together.
We could say we hurt each other, but
would that even feel true now? You,
on a flight to Mexico, the grace of four
Alaska winters already behind you, a life
you could've only found without
me. I can't say it feels good
that it didn't work out, can only say
that there's no path on offer I'd take
if it meant I'd lose your friendship,
your deep laugh a staircase of
seven stories, seven years we walked
together. In a world where broken
romance tells us that one person must
be wrong and the other damaged,
how is it that I now love you more whole?
You are no longer my ex-girlfriend; you
are the heart that holds the fullest knowing
of my youth, the years we thought we knew,
but didn't.

BRIEF, MOSTLY AIR

When?

To what expanding end?
What lung bloated with laugh
decided to send you to me?

A full smile across the breakfast table.
No, not light.
Not something given and wide and warm, like what a fire leaves behind.
More like the word for fire.

Brief. Mostly air. An unexpected lift
from the flint of lip – that ends in a growl.
If it ends.

Seven weeks now, I've been dating you.
Someone in my life, some friend of a friend
or friend of my mother's, when I was furnishing
my heartbreak as if I would stay there awhile,
said maybe things would not get better but that they would
change.

It was the right thing to say.

I think of you and smile, a little more fond
of breaking. The fact of it. How it also takes a mouth open,
a flick of the tongue to say *love*. One night,
I step out into your courtyard and watch a racoon plunder
the trash, his moonbit eyes pause on me –

he leaps into the darkness, where he lands –
or doesn't – on the other

side.

HER FIRST TIME

All thumbs have their own angle, orientation. Yours
are tabletops that could hold tiny tea parties, booths jutting
from the divey breakfast joints of your palms.
Your fingers delicately spin around them as you unbutton
your blouse, December air and nerves lift your skin into tiny
effigy mounds. I am skittish, too. You wonder if it is possible to love
a woman and I wonder if it is possible to not be hurt
by one. We both get our answer.

BABY GAY OF CLIFDEN

You were the first to not know enough
to want to hide me. To others, I was something

they always knew was in the house somewhere,
the one they could visualize in different places – the

junk drawer? the garage? the closet? under
the sink?– but couldn't seem to place.

You didn't know enough to put me away
for later. You were delighted that I was there,

a mirror you passed every time you went to the kitchen,
out in the open, a beautiful glass, and I thought

this must be what it is when someone loves you.
I thought *this must be what it is like to be seen,*

but really, you just didn't know enough to be ashamed
of the reflection. When we say *queer*

we mean the times our fathers made us bleed,
how we have learned to grasp hands like a tangled necklace

when someone stares in the street, to not let go
even as they try to unravel us. We mean queer like

you better call the jeweler if you want to keep this chain,
and when you came to know this word

outside the confines of our clandestine romance,
the knowing was an ocean.

I understand the sea legs of your heart, my dear. I was happy
to row you out. You don't know enough

to want to keep me
and I am a far worse teacher than water.

I'll miss you,
I'll miss you,
I'll miss you.

YOU ARE THE ONLY ONE TO ASK ME TO STAY, AND I DIDN'T

I wintered with you,
where others have sought you
in your spring, your heart season, your late summer
drip, pastures a soft green pan of biscuits,
I arrived in a metallic sheen (it was cold
that year, wasn't it?). We were broken
in the opposite direction: you, from attempting to feel
too little and me, from feeling it all at once.
You sounded like a walk through
a forest of twigs; loud and dead.
We talked and everything you said was

what do I do with myself now that I can't drink
without dying

and when we fucked you got angry when I tried
to look you in the eye. Solstice always comes,
you little blonde tremble. The waxing moon, a lid
opening to see. It is bright though it cannot warm.
I can't tell you who you are
without liquor and you can't tell me who I am
without love. We can both let go and wait
for the sun.

CASUAL DATING

Today a lover asked me what I was looking
for after we had already taken off our clothes.
I felt self-conscious - do I kiss like someone
who has lost something? Did I rifle through her,
a dresser drawer stuffed with things I never
wear? The truth was in there somewhere,
the question *is there danger of you loving me
too much?* Yes, I would go back to holding her
and not knowing she'd hidden the steak knife
under the pillow, but no, there isn't anything
for you to worry about now that I understand
someone can want to hurt me on purpose.

PRAISE KINK

Like the long lineage of queers before me,

I explore kink in the bedroom. It's like this;   some people will use your old name
and pronouns to your face because they believe in God

instead of you. Your friend will correct herself in person but join the seance of your
friends and family back home

who miss your dead self. Or it's like this;   one ex-fiancé will always be visibly
drunk while telling you she isn't,

and keep a list of your flaws in her wallet to look at every time she feels lonely.

There's an ex that took five years to convince you to date them,

then when they touched you it felt like they were cleaning a mirror.   My therapist
said there's no wrong reason to explore new desire. Even if it's because I find it
refreshing to know

when people want to hurt me in advance? Yes, even then.

Good girl.

A FEMME TO HER BUTCH

I said, "Here, love, break me of this chomping rage."
I said, "Take me from this bullshit, this ever-expanding echo
of unfair with your take-out teriyaki, unfair with my next gimlet,
your *rí rá agus ruaille buaille* next to my mop & broom."
Resting has always been my way of getting even.
I have brought the requisite light touch to so many crisp
& delicate mascs & the way they needed the lighting *just so*,
swept up their hair after I trimmed the edges – the whole
merciless drudgery of straightness we fall into unsanctioned, without ever noticing.
I paint my eyelashes & grow my hair & so you forget
I am queer & not a Wife Lite. But my dear, should we dream
of anything, let's dream ourselves away from this:
this world of men that sees us as silly children playing house,
swallowing both feet.

JULY 31ST, 2021

We bumped upper arms every few steps as we left the bar,
two lone balloons after the party, tied together, caught

in a shy dance. Tiny hairs lifted off our skin, reaching for one another
under an immense poverty of touch. This was the summer

we pretended like nothing would come of it; we would not feel
a full year's loss of smile. We could hear the keening

of the music we left in the distance, smoker hollers from the street,
puddles splitting themselves for passing cars. Almost normal

sounds, but sadder: an extinction nostalgia. I had to leave
the next day, & back then, we still didn't trust anything we knew

would be coming back. I did not tell myself then, but I was in love
with you almost immediately. You asked me to climb a tree,

it's safer up here, & we talked on separate branches, two feet closer
than we ought. I wonder at it all: how I followed you up without question,

how we weighed kissing with dying & knew if we didn't
we already were.

50

SWALLOW

Did you see it, its belly lit by the setting light, as it tilted
and swooped above our heads? Did you see three more
of them, rising and falling in the golden air, tiny specs
of white flight, a perfect ruckus of glitter creatures as they leaned into
the rudders of their wings: a sky lake, a ripple glistening its way between trees?
And did you feel it, in your heart, how they meant everything?
Have you realized that even though they know nothing about
our love, they know what it is for? And what will we decide
to do with it, now that we sit here tangled beneath the
sugar gum tree, both wanting to be chosen, neither knowing
if we should?

WHY I AM NO LONGER A LESBIAN

My father always used to tell me the story of my name. How close of a tie it was between Claire and Erin, Maureen and Casey. It is the first thing I learned to respond to: this word that could've been any word. Later, I took on so many other words: rebellious, morose, lesbian, poet. How did I know then that those things mattered? This Pride, my mother mentioned how wonderful it must

be to not have to hide as a lesbian these days. How it isn't a *big deal* anymore. I don't ask her to use my correct pronouns, or tell her every gender I call myself is a mismatched sock and I hope every person I fuck is the missing one under the couch cushions. I say I do not explain it because she is 74 years old, but it is probably more because I remember 2006. When

lesbian was certainly a *big deal* to her. My cousin called me from a college party one night to tell me he was gay, but said not to tell the family. *I would never,* I replied. I was pushed down a flight of stairs to become the person he knew to call. Later, my nephew and niece would take me to lunch to tell me their own taps on the shoulder. *I am pansexual. I am gay.* Their arrival into

queerness had nothing to do with my name, but everything to do with being called something. When you ask me how I came to name myself, what I am called, of course I do not have a short answer. I have 15 years of story to explain a large scar on my feet from walking down Highway 36 barefoot, bleeding, freshly thrown from my childhood home.

Why did I call myself a *lesbian*? Because it's who I was. Because it is a name I nearly died for. But I did not know that I would love you then. All I know of who I am is through the ones I've loved. I have no idea if I can live up to the person I'll learn I am from you, but I will call myself anything that holds us both fully. So what does this make me now, if not a

lesbian? More. A throat of birds. Neck nest. The words I say fly, they become. How would I not name myself from how I feel about you? For this is what I know: your mouth ignites this chirping heart, and that song is what I am.

T4T (TRANS 4 TRANS)

I.   The night before your first testosterone shot,
your mouth negotiates with the parts of my body
that throw white flags to the world – the traitors. You call
me perfect, & I know exactly who you mean. Tomorrow,
I will pinch your thigh & hold the bridge of myself steady
between you & your right blood.

II.   The insurance company says I am not trans enough
for my surrender to be anything but cosmetic,
& I cannot afford to be not trans enough. I have looked
into a thousand mirrors & never once felt seen,
my skin a tomb I walk around in waiting for the air
to run out. I have spent my life digging holes, chosen lovers
for their shovels. When you tell me you'd recognize me anywhere,
I know exactly who you mean.

III.   Isn't love so uncertain? It is through this den of
trepidation that we breathe. We create all the right confusion
in the right people. I'm learning how to be
unsure & trusting. I'm learning how to ask
your body who you are every day. Let what is right
enter us & move the muscle & fat from our hips.
Let the surgeons cut smiles into your chest
& under my belly. We will reinvent our bodies.

IV.   They'll ask us who we are & the answer will be
that we love each other. We are becoming what we are
& we are what we are all at once. & don't we love it
like that? Don't I love all of you at once?

WHERE THE STARS FINALLY REACH US

Smell the jasmine draped over the side gate
                        a cenote pools between your breasts
the open windows valve   for the air we thicken
            salt lamp extends the dusk   past midnight
                        with its pink glow
                        and we are still laughing
where things start
is predictable
                        the nerves
                        are at the end of things
                                    my pinky finger stretches
                                        in rebellion to my shy palm, hooks itself
                                    into yours
pulls you in to touch lips
                        where the world crackles, reaches itself toward
                                                    the implausible always
                        didn't we talk about those NASA photos?
            how one galaxy holds
                        another that holds
                                    a planet that holds
                                                this little house on 66th
                                                where you hold
                                                        me
blanketed in everything
                        so small
                                    where the stars finally reach us

THEY SAY IT'S THE LITTLE THINGS,
AND THEY AREN'T WRONG

A snoring dog wakes me. I reach over you for the glass that lives on your bedside
table: the one that is never washed and sits gathering

limestone rings from thirsts forgotten. The hard heel in me soaks, softening to see
you've sacrificed a small grievance to my oft chaotic sleep.

You would, of course, prefer that I go downstairs, pull a clean mason jar from
the cupboard, press it against the white lip of the dispenser, and drink

from there. Put it in the dishwasher when I'm done. But you know me well.
I will sooner go thirsty for the full length of darkness before I disturb

the slumberous curlicue of a pup at my feet. You have seen me languish of a dry mouth
beneath the warm thrum of her breath: my discomfort a quiet, unnecessary gift.

And so you leave the glass in its nettlesome state. After a lifetime of predictable dusks,
this care for me is a morning that licks a hanky and kneels to rub the crusts

from our long love's eyes. I look at you dozing fresh-faced, honey-mooned as
our first July kiss. So many had given no ease for my throat when it was raw

in front of them. Yet you leave me a corner of convenient filth every time you wish
to tidy the bedroom, and guard even my most senseless sweetness with a small comfort.

A LESSON ON CAPITALISM
FROM A MOSQUITO

It is the season of wet.   Sog creeps,

turns branches into doughy veins   & the belly sun

tilts itself into an orange southern pour.   A neon algae bloom

curdles beneath the heat and,   for some, this is birth.

I like to chase the world down   hungry & quickonly

stopping to eat.   I do all things with intent:

hatch, pupate,   seek & desire.

                              You see work

as obligatory, exhausting.   Maybe

it is the lack of a proboscis,   or being forced to toil

in order to earn rest - your species' tiring march

of labor buckling in on itself.   But real work

has a song -   a single note hum that alerts the world

it is you, & you are here -   a frequency born in idleness,

bred from rot,   that will only subside

when you are truly fed.

AMERICA THE SPECTACLE

I.
My mother bends a hanger into an antenna
        to watch her favorite soap opera, the television
        a ghost with ears. You only know America from inside
        that box. So what is my country to you?
        An afternoon drama?

II.
In one episode, I reach my hand out –
        palm brushing along golden rows of grain.
        I kiss a girl with buckwheat hair, lips soaked
        with sun. It is almost perfect.
        I was told there's a dream
        while rubbing two pennies together for heat.
        Here, dreams aren't how you make fire –
        money is.

III.
So what is your country to me?
        She's carving one of her neighbor's turnips,
        giving it eyes and teeth. I am looking out –
        a burning coal. She chisels ears for me.
        She says to you, *look*
        at the ones who turned flames to coin,
        how they live in the box
        for eternity.

HERE IS THE POEM ABOUT HOME

I.
The tap water is so loaded with lime
there's a white dust around all of the faucets;

It drives S crazy, this house,

M knows the intricacies of the coffee maker
and I make it so poorly one morning that we all may as well be drinking a cup
of the Silver Strand. I never make it

again. It isn't that we all are falling out of the pants we once wore –
we are getting older, we met old –

or that the front room is filled with instruments we've only played together once.
The difference between everyone and us, we say, is we welcome our magic,

write our ideas on a blackboard, talk about which ones
will make us rich. Mostly we sit silently sipping

our tea next to the fire in the living room, as three hounds snore
at our feet.

II.
I still recall driving past the town my great-grandparents left to come to America.
It doesn't really exist
anymore. I have cousins who are likely uninterested in me.

I visited a tree in Westport, or it asked me to call in,
and though I'd never napped beneath a tree before (Imagine! A poet never having
done this),

I dozed on the green moss on its legs. When I got home,

a heaving sadness overtook me. I knew that it wasn't mine.
I was grateful to be trusted with it.

III.
Nothing lasts forever, unless everything does.

I am either a woman returning home or she is buried in Boston.

IV.
My mother
was never given enough grace,
was given a life heavier than iron,
one that was hard to love, and
she struggled to hold it in one hand and
her children in another.

It is not a lack of love that makes me unwilling to take it from her.
It is that I can now give her one arm free

so she may offer her own strength back to it.

V.
There almost weren't any instruments. Almost wasn't a great-grandmother tree.

Just the capital of Connemara and a love I'll never forget. Soft river crossings.
A big triangle building we said we'd get married in someday. But she left me and

it sent me east. A lifetime isn't long enough to thank her for that.

VI.
I accept that I have sister griefs to tend to. That I am in love with a country so
madly that my tongue cannot

lay flat enough to deliver its sweetness.

TELLING THE PEOPLE WHO MADE YOUR BODY
IT IS THE WRONG BODY

I step across the words,
the small wounds
of phrase,
to lay the swaddle
of my transness down,
knowing it is
an unintended birth.
Accidents recognize
other accidents,
always.
I perch between one self
& another,
from my stout
& happenstance born-body
that my mother &
father insist
they still know –
      me, a child
      that has not managed
      to repay the debt of my life –
to the voice carrying me
that says
your body is not a hotel
you can check in and out of,
you must make it
home.

I AM A TRANS PERSON FROM THE US STATE THAT INVENTED MASS SHOOTINGS

In my new home 1500 miles away, I sit on the toilet after waking at 5am with terrible pain. Nothing moves through me - my gut churns and holds on like I'm apt to do with much of my sickness. I open my phone to distract myself, let go. BREAKING NEWS, it says, and I vomit on my own feet.

There's not a single poem without love in it. Even in this story, where I drag the still-warm bits of my stomach through the carpet to the bedroom, unable to bother with a towel. Readers will know this unfathomable secret of mine - that I was led by my own acrid breath to the side of my partner and shook them awake to make sure we were both alive. That I sat thinking *it could've been us* when it already was someone.

We were alive, and it brings no solace to the poem. We were alive, and there is love. But here it is turned upside down. It is what I imagine the light from a disco ball looks like reflected in your own blood. How it keeps spinning on its glittered axis even after the fluorescents turn on to let the paramedics in. How the rainbow lights swap for red and blue through the only window.

Here is where Mary Oliver would discuss an egret or curled snake in a grassland outside Monument, the creature indifferent to gender living its beautiful, thoughtless life. Here is where the metaphor would go. But a trans man named Daniel is dead, and I was just considering a haircut like his for myself last weekend.

THE IMPOSSIBLE EXPLANATION OF LIGHT
after Mary Oliver

I thought the shadow remembered me, she took me back so tenderly at first.
She arranged her pleated trousers, her pockets stuffed with long yawns and
discarded feathers. I curled into her and collected the most sleep I'd found

in years, each wave of dream washing up another softened shard of sea glass,
as if nothing but choice stood between me and the whole colorful glass jar
of death. But my hopes, she did not recognize them, or you. All night

I tried to explain the small kingdoms breathing in my new, courageous life;
the summer crickets' friction a crooning night song, our own legs rubbing together
beneath the sheets to lull the luminous world to bed with us. How being

alive and trans and in love was not just a miracle, but the most natural thing
on earth. By morning I had vanished at least a dozen times into longing,
a return to you the unspoken inevitable, the explanation of light

impossible.

IT IS MY QUEER NAME-GIVING

I start to undress my skull.
A ribbon of long, black hair falls
like an alias revealed.
I giggle and touch myself
where I am now naked.
Everything I've been called before
was a whisper
and this is the sensation
of loud. I am a curtain
on opening night. I drag the clippers
from temple to spine and
my hand grows numb with the rumble
of the razor's applause. That which covered me
pools at my feet. Parts of me arrive
that haven't been seen before: a mole
above my ear that has never been kissed,
a startling dash of untanned skin,
the pulse from that fierce New Mexico morning I woke in her arms
and knew that this was the only way
for me to love. I rub my hand over my head,
the texture of new down. I curl into
my palm. I say my name.
The last of it falls away,
I say
my name.

ACKNOWLEDGMENTS

Thank you to the journals, anthologies, and publications where the following poems were published in previous iterations, occasionally under different titles:

"On Loss" and "It Is My Queer Name-Giving," *Pile Press*, Issue 1, August 2021

"Love Doesn't Hurt," *Impossible Archetype*, Issue 10, August 2021

"Poppy," "The Nights of Lost Cause," "Baby Gay of Clifden," "You Are The Only One To Ask Me To Stay, and I Didn't" *Hole in the Head Review*, No. 3, Issue 1, February 2022

"Car Tattoo" *Banshee Lit*, 13th Issue, 2022

"Why I Am No Longer a Lesbian" *Poetry Ireland Review*, Issue 136, 2022

"Cuir Oideachas ar do Mhac (Educate Your Sons)" *Howl: New Irish Writing*, October 2022

"Modern Miracle" *HAD*, July 2022

"July 31, 2021" *Oxford Poetry*, Issue 94

"T4T (Trans 4 Trans)" Renard Press, *Spectrum Poetry Anthology*

"Misophonia, or How To Be Trans & Be Quiet" *Lucky Jefferson*, 365 Collection

The final line in "Cuir Oideachas ar do Mhac (Educate Your Sons)" is an adaptation of a co-written line in "Flowers of Hiroshima" by the Denver Mercury Cafe Slam Team of 2009, of which I was a member.

To all those who I have imperfectly loved and who have imperfectly loved me - I am so grateful to you.

To Jordan, who has brought vibrancy, laughter, hope, and support to my life in a way I never thought possible.

To my parents, who were raised in an entirely different time and given a completely opposing set of values but have never stopped fighting to be in my life. They went through their own dark nights while I went through mine, and we have hurt one another in occasionally unfathomable ways. But I count myself so lucky, because every bit of turmoil has been worth the love and support they have never once stopped trying to provide. To my sisters Andrea and Katie, who I never doubt for one second love me and will always be there for me, who I miss all the time, who are my best friends for life. To my nephews and niece (and new great nephew!) – Mason, Hayden, Collin, Gia, Evan, Eli, Kayden, and Donny – who are way cooler than me. To my aunt Kay, whose love of God and family radiates through everything she does, who has never ceased supporting me and loving me – thank you.

To my family across the pond – to Stephanie and Mark, who let me, a relative stranger, into their home, poured me baths and negronis, and have since provided me with their creative partnerships in ways I only ever dreamed. This book would literally not exist without them – I wrote half of it in their home, read first drafts over the dinner table, and have sent countless edits and voice notes over WhatsApp. To my Aunt Teri, who showed me around Westport and pulled me angel cards and helped me talk to my cousin again across the great expanse of souls, so that I could eventually find my own beneath a tree near the quay. To Sarah, who never fails to listen and understand and advise in the most gracious and kind way. To Fiadh and Ciarán, with whom I shared the stage, and who I watch in awe of their poetic creativity and wisdom. To Jensen, Brody, Eszter, Aoibín, and Ana, for all the letters and insta banter and support. To Jacob, my musical genius of a friend, old prom date, who watched me yell with an accidentally strange accent at an old landlord in Cork – I am so grateful to have reconnected with you and can't wait to see where our friendship goes from here. For anyone not named here, know it is truly through ADHD accident that you're not listed, and my appreciation knows no bounds.

To my poetic mentors – Bhanu Kapil, Sierra DeMulder, Denver slam poets circa 2007-2010 – Ayinde Russel, Lindsay McGuire, Ian Dogherty, Paulie Lipman, Bianca Shaw, Ladyspeech Sankofa, Jen Rinaldi, Rebecca Preston, Amy Everhart, Suzi Q Smith. Thank you for your kindness and patience with me during that time in my life - when I was young and passionate, but reckless and ignorant. Thank you for all you taught me. It was a formative time in my life and I owe much to you and the community.

To my friends in the States who in various ways informed or edited or advised me in my work - Chantelle, Sophia, Olivia, Ashton, Victoria, Danielle, Abbie, Carter, Danni, Connor, Leah, all the Thembos (Annika, Mila, Nelle), and more. If you aren't listed and we are buds, again - ADHD, and thank you.

To the fellow survivors who suffered narcissistic abuse from the same person that I did - you saved my life in those few months after I got out with your solidarity, text messages, and emails. Thank you for your bravery in being willing to talk to me, and for your bravery in surviving. I'll never forget you.

To my queer and trans family across the globe - you are beautiful, you are worthy of being seen and heard, and you make life worth living. Our existence is resistance - keep fighting.

Finally, to my new Write Bloody UK family - I am so lucky to get to join you on this wild journey. Thank you for believing in this book.

ABHAINN CONNOLLY (they/them) is a trans and queer poet that splits their time between Drogheda, Ireland and the Pacific Northwest of the USA. Their written work can be found in esteemed Irish & UK literary journals like *Poetry Ireland Review*, *Banshee Lit*, and *Oxford Poetry*, as well as US publishers like *HAD*, *Frontier*, and *Hole in the Head Review*. They were a finalist for the Jack McCarthy Book Prize in 2021 (Write Bloody) and longlisted for the Frontier New Voices Contest 2022.

Find them online @meabhainn and www.abhainnconnolly.com

If you like Abhainn Connolly,
Abhainn Connolly likes...

What We Are Given
OLLIE O'NEIL

Floating Brilliant Gone
FRANNY CHOI

Every Little Vanishing
SHELEEN McELHINNEY

Counting Descent
CLINT SMITH

New Shoes On A Dead Horse
SIERRA DeMULDER

Bloody beautiful books.

Write Bloody UK is an independent poetry publisher passionate about bringing the voices of UK poets to the masses. Trailing after Write Bloody Publishing (US) and Write Bloody North (Canada), we are committed to handling the creation, distribution and marketing of our authors; binding their words in beautiful, velvety-to-the-touch books and touring loudly with them through UK cities.

Support independent authors, artists and presses.

Want to know more about Write Bloody UK books, authors, and events?
Join our mailing list at:

WWW.WRITEBLOODYUK.CO.UK

More Write Bloody UK Books

Milton Keynes UK
Ingram Content Group UK Ltd.
UKHW011942240823
427447UK00004B/49